FOREST BOOKS

LET'S TALK ABOUT THE WEATHER...
AND OTHER POEMS

Marin Sorescu was born in the village of
Bulzeşti, county of Dolj, the fifth child of a
family of peasants. He attended secondary
schools in Craiova and Predeal, graduating
from Iaşi University with a B.A. in Philo-
logy. Since 1978 he has been working as
editor-in-chief of the literary review
'Ramuri'.

His first volume of poetry SINGUR
PRINTRE POEŢI (Alone amongst Poets)
appeared in 1964, followed by numerous
volumes of poetry, prose and drama.

In 1974 he was awarded the prize for
drama by the Writers' Union of Romania
and in 1978 the international prize Le
Muze by the Academia delle Muze,
Florence. In 1983 he was made a corres-
pondent member of the "Mallarmé"
Academy in Paris and in December of the
same year he received the International
Poetry Prize "Fernando Riello" in
Madrid.

His work has been translated into most
languages and his plays performed
throughout the world.

For Dennis and Jolyon

LET'S TALK
ABOUT
THE
WEATHER . . .

AND OTHER POEMS BY
MARIN SORESCU

TRANSLATED
by
ANDREA DELETANT
and
BRENDA WALKER

Introduction
POET TO POET
by
JON SILKIN

FOREST BOOKS
LONDON * 1985 * BOSTON

Published by FOREST BOOKS
20 Forest View, Chingford, London E4 7AY, U.K.
61 Lincoln Road, Wayland, MA. 01788, U.S.A.

First published 1985

Typeset in Great Britain by Cover to Cover, Cambridge
Printed in Great Britain by A. Wheaton & Co. Ltd., Exeter

Jacket design © Ann Evans
Translations © Andrea Deletant, Brenda Walker

British Library Cataloguing in Publication Data
Sorescu, Marin
Let's talk about the weather – and other poems by Marin Sorescu.
I. Title
859'.134   PC840.29.074
ISBN 0-9509487-8-0

Library of Congress Catalog Card Number
85-070247

Contents

Marin Sorescu assisted the translators in the selection of these poems

Introduction

Poet to Poet

Wit in the early eighteenth-century poetry of England is a different article from wit as we understand it now. If we situate it between the quick centre of metaphor of the seventeenth-century metaphysical poets, and the active imagination that Coleridge reserved for the poetry he valued, that approaches its character. The wondering alert metaphors of Donne and Herbert are often touched with both humour and good humour, and the strong physical component in their metaphors balances up the idea in its abstract nature. There is no earth-bound soul that can be without a body. A world of matter and soul, each divided from and bound to the other.

Wit of this kind is what, equivalently, Sorescu often uses, and it gives the poems most of their attributes. At their best they possess a stringent intelligence, a wry pained humour, invention, and a placing of insight in concise imagery. The imagery has what Eliot in his remarks on Jonson's poetry termed 'profile'. The purity of outline suited Eliot very well, and it also serves to help Sorescu get his image out cleanly without needing to bother as much with resonance.

The same source of Sorescu's strength is, perhaps paradoxically, that of his weakness. He sometimes sacrifices too much to inventiveness; his work being at times deft, yet occasionally, despite overt disclaimers in his verse, lacking heart.

What makes Sorescu a poet, however – in the translations, which are my only means of reading his work – is not just the metaphysical imagination, but, at his best, an unlikely coupling of this mode with sensuous power.

Here are a few instances of Sorescu's invention.

In 'Eyes', these organs will enlarge until 'I will be nothing but a black dot/in their midst'; then they allow all the phenomenon of the visible universe to enter them. Through these evidences of the external world, the poet sees that world. The tension between the seeing and the seen is resolved in a fusion of ego and external reality – of self with what is not self. Invention is kept in check by modesty, and out of respect for what is other than self.

In 'The Gift' there is narrative strength, and in 'Carbon Paper' imaginative wit is placed in imagery familiar to us as moderns:

> At night someone puts on my door
> A huge carbon paper,
> And all my thoughts appear, instantaneously
> On the outside of the door.

Perhaps there is here a political undertone, familiar enough East of the Curtain, but also legible in the West with its own passion for files on dissident individuals.

In 'Look' we do not read an idea, or even an idea clothed in imagery; the sensuousness is an essential part of the character of the idea:

> Someone understood you for a moment
> Making your name
> Pass through your body,
> Painful and sonorous,
> Like a bronze tongue
> Through the emptiness of a bell.

Identity and respect for another's identity and person, have become crucial issues in the twentieth century. It is an age which appears to sanction the notion that large populations of people are, in the heap, valueless ciphers. One's name, it is true, is not one's character, but it is an essential sign of identity. The devalued individual and that person's body is made empty, like a bell; therefore the name that tolls through it is exaggerated in compensation for this devaluation and emptiness. The emptiness itself exaggerates the clang. Thus 'Painful and sonorous'. This is Sorescu in a fine passage, showing not telling, as the current cliché says.

In 'If it's not asking too much', God replies to his human suppliant with 'You do ask too much'. The humour resides in the traces of irritation with which we see the Divine respond. A comparable exchange, with a similar sense of irritation, is conveyed in the episode between God, Sarah and Abraham in Genesis 18, 10–15. Funnier, indeed, than Sorescu; although Sorescu is witty enough.

Sorescu, like many modern poets, comments on poetry and its social role. In 'Thieves' the allegory of art as an article of goodness, and as a potentially healing agent, is created:

And the same for each new poem.
A good soul was found to receive it.

Firmness of outline need not preclude a complex interpenetration of imagery. In 'The Camel' there is such an exchange, and in 'Deeply Cerebral' there is a beautiful apprehension of the sources of creation, of which love is one instance and art another. This is perhaps Sorescu at his best. The wit and humour are kept in right tension with the sensuousness without one diminishing the other. On the contrary, each is enriched by contact with the other:

As we got dressed in this state of fusion,
This downpour of angels,
Spindles of smoke dripping in stanzas,
The soul in holes − hexagons, hexagons,
A honeycomb for smoke.
The smoke's our honey.
This honeycomb presumes a melody the soul touches
Perfecting, making it geometrical . . .

I missed you like a trajectory in a void, in longing,
Dressed in decoration, in any way,
I simply missed you, the way you are, *tale quale.*
I got used to passing there
On that trajectory
And with you the void seemed heavy
With astral beauty.

Two last instances. In 'Sentence' the wit is almost an impudence, its declaration impossible of realization in its literalness. We find this elsewhere in for instance, Magritte's work; consider the painting 'La Vie secrete', where a man faces a mirror which reflects the back of his head and trunk. With 'The Old Ones in the Shade' we re-create, in reading, a place of strange identity, the oddness of which suggests that Sorescu not only knows the place but also inhabits it. It is a place where heat and age belong:

The sultry heat resembles old age,
The same sensations.

That unlikely equivalence or interconnection is not mere oddity; it is oddity, and produces verse of an unfamiliar sensation.

x

The range, so far as this selection of Sorescu's poems is concerned, is not wide, but there is considerable intensity; and where he is not tempted to make minimal art and *avert* his sensuous powers, there is a human strength and vision. It is these last that extend what seems to be the limitations imposed by his powers of wit. That capacity to extend one's limits we usually term growth, and that, I think, is one of Sorescu's hidden preoccupations, even if, ostensibly, the poems appear to endorse the familiar wry and modern version of wisdom through experience. Wisdom implies, often, understandably enough, an acceptance of the status quo. Growth would appear to set it aside.

Jon Silkin

THE ROAD

Pensive and with hands behind my back
I'm walking on the tracks,
The straightest road
There is.

From behind me, at speed,
Comes a train
Which hasn't yet heard of me.

This train – Old Zen be my witness –
Will never, ever reach me,
Because I'll always be ahead
Of things that don't think.

Or even if brutally
It should pass over me,
There'll always be someone
Who'll be walking ahead of it
Full of thought,
Hands behind his back.

Like me now
In front of the black monster
Which approaches with frightening speed
And which will never, ever
Reach me.

THE SNAIL

The snail has covered his eyes firmly
With wax,
Has put his head on his chest
And stares
Into himself.

Above him
Is the shell –
His perfect creation
Of which he is sick and tired –

Around the shell
Is the world,
The rest of the world,
Set out this way and that
According to certain laws
Of which he's sick and tired –

And in the centre of this
Universal sickness
There is the snail
Himself
Of whom he's sick and tired.

HYMN

Instead of roots, trees have
Saints,
Risen from the table
To kneel beneath the earth
In prayer.

Only their haloes
Are left above,
These trees,
These flowers.

And we in turn,
Will be saints,
Praying the earth
Stays round and blessed
Always.

3

FRAMES

The walls of my house are covered
In frames
In which my friends
See nothing.
They think I put them there
To annoy them.

There's one gap left
Above the bed,
And I wake with a strange
Feeling
Of being watched.

In fact, on that spot
The light plays
In spherical patterns.

But there's no bulb there,
No open eye,
No phosphorous mine.

Yet despite all this
Above the bed
Someone breathes, breathes.

Who knows what star burns
Far away,
And by the strange law of reflections
Its soul now beats
Upon my wall.

Tomorrow I must put
A frame there
As well.

4

CREATION

I'm writing on earthquakes
And if some words
Slip a lot further over
Only the crust of the earth is at fault
With its lack of stability.

You can never tell
When a volcano might erupt beneath your desk
And after a day's work
You could be signing on ash.

Everything changes
Place.
The lamp from the ceiling comes under my chin,
The mountain from the horizon comes into my mouth.
A gag whose remains
Will still be spat out
By my descendants of the seventh family down.

The leaves from the tree tops
Have all moved underground
For fear of earthquakes.

Many, many ancestors of mine
Have moved underground
For fear of earthquakes.

Only I still try to connect
Like lines after a derailment
These two words,
Which run, one in one direction,
And one in the other
Mad with terror.

TRANSLATION

I was taking an exam
In a dead language,
And had to translate myself
From man into monkey.

I started in a roundabout way
First translating a text
From a forest.

However, the closer I got to myself,
The more and more difficult
The translation became.
With a little effort
I found those satisfactory equivalents
For toe nails and hair on legs.

At about the knees
I began to stammer,
At the heart my hand shook
And I made a blot on the sun.

I tried to improve it
With the hair on my chest.
But finally stumbled
At the soul.

THE WHISTLE

A whistle suddenly shrieks
Behind a passer-by
And his body fills with sawdust
Like a tree, at the edge of the forest,
When it senses
The saw.

Better not turn round – he says to himself –
Perhaps it's for someone else.
Anyway, let's have a breathing space
For a few more steps.

The piercing whistle
Is heard behind every passer-by
Who turns purple, yellow, greed, red
And continues walking rigidly onwards,
Without turning round.
It must be for someone else –
Everybody thinks –
What have I done apart from
One war, two?
Tomorrow I'm getting married,
The day after tomorrow my wife gives birth –
The day after that I'm burying my parents –
I've got so much to worry about,
It can't possibly be for me.

A child,
Who bought himself a whistle,
Had come outside to try it
On the street,
Wickedly whistling in the ear of the people.

LATE

It's beginning to get late in me.
Look, it's grown dark in my right hand
And in the acacia at the front of the house.
I must put out with an eyelid
All things which stayed alight,
The slippers near the bed,
The hallstand, the paintings.
As for the rest of life's belongings,
Everything that can be seen,
Even beyond the stars,
There's no point in taking those with me,
They'll continue to burn.
And in the remembrance of me
I've left word
That at least on more important feast days,
The whole universe be given to the world
As alms.

CHESS

I move a white day,
He moves a black,
I advance with a dream.
He takes it to war.
He attacks my lungs,
I think for about a year in hospital.
I make a brilliant combination
And win a black day.
He moves a disaster
And threatens me with cancer
(which moves for the moment in the shape of a cross)
But I put a book before him
He's obliged to retreat.
I win a few more pieces,
But, look, half my life
Is taken.
— If I give you check, you lose your optimism,
He tells me,
— It doesn't matter, I joke,
I'll do the castling of feelings,

Behind me my wife, children.
The sun, the moon and other onlookers
Tremble for every move I make.

I light a cigarette
And continue the game.

ANGLE

Hands were placed over his eyes
And he was shown the world,
A large drawing
On a screen.

– What's this letter?
He was asked.
– Night, he replied,
– You're wrong, it's the sun.
Everyone knows there are no rays
At night. Now this one?
– Night.
– Don't make me laugh!
It's the sea, how could there be
Such darkness at sea?
Now this one?
The man hesitated a little,
Then replied,
– Night.
– But it's a woman.
Night hasn't breasts, you know,
You've obviously been misled
By the black hair. Now this one?
Look at it carefully
Before you reply.
– It's still the night.
– A pity you haven't guessed right this time either,

That letter there was
You.

Next!

THE ILLNESS

I can feel something dying, Doctor,
It's just here around my being,
All my inside hurts,
During the day it's the sun that hurts,
And at night it's the moon and the stars.

I get a sharp pain in the cloud on the sky
Which I didn't even notice until today,
And I wake up every morning
With a sort of winter feeling.

I've taken all kinds of medicine, but it's done no good,
I've hated, and loved, I learned to read,
And I even read some books,
I talked to people and had a think,
I was good and I was handsome . . .

But none of it did any good, Doctor,
And I've spent no end of years on it.

I think I must have caught death
One day
When I was born.

EYES

My eyes are growing larger and larger,
Like two circles of water
They have covered all my forehead
And half my chest.
Before long they will be as large
As me.

Larger than me,
Much larger than me:
I will be nothing but a black dot
In their midst.

And so as not to feel lonely,
I'll let many, many things
Into their circle:
The moon, the sun, woods and seas
With which I'll go on looking
At the world.

SHAKESPEARE

Shakespeare created the world in seven days.

On the first day he made the sky, the mountains and the depths
of the soul.
On the second day he made rivers, seas, oceans
And other emotions —
And he gave them to Hamlet, Julius Ceasar, Anthony, Cleopatra
and Ophelia,
To Othello and others,
To be master over them, with their descendants,
For ever and ever.
On the third day he gathered all the people
And taught them to savour:
The taste of happiness, love, despair,
The taste of jealousy, fame and so on,
Until all tasting was finished.
Then some late-comers arrived.
The creator patted their heads with compassion,
Saying the only roles left for them were
The literary critics
Who could then demolish his work.
The fourth and fifth day he reserved for laughter.
He allowed clowns
To tumble,
He allowed kings, emperors
And other unfortunates to amuse themselves.
On the sixth day he completed the administration:
He set up a tempest,
He taught King Lear
How to wear a straw crown.
As there were a few leftovers from the creation of the world
He designed Richard III.
On the seventh day he took stock to see what else might be done.
And Shakespeare thought that after so much effort
He deserved to see a performance.
But first, as he was overtired,
He went to die a little.

TWICE

I look at everything
Twice,
Once to be cheerful
And once to be sad.

Trees have a peal of laughter
In their crown of leaves
And a large tear
In the roots.
The sun is young
At the tip of its rays
But the rays
Are implanted in night.

The world is enclosed perfectly
Between these two covers
Where I've crammed everthing
I've loved
Twice.

THE SHELL

I'm hidden in a shell on the bottom of the sea,
But I've forgotten which.

Daily I go down to the deep
And seive it through my fingers
To find myself.

Sometimes I think
A huge fish has eaten me
And now I search everywhere
To help it swallow the rest.

The bottom of the sea attracts and terrifies me
With its millions of shells
All so alike.

Good people, I am in one of these
But I don't know which.

The number of times I went straight up to one
Saying "This is me."
But when I opened the shell
It was empty.

THE FOUNDATION

The way you stand
Upright,
With soft arms
On your full womb,
You seem the wife
Of a ruler from ancient times
Holding their founded church.

And I can almost hear a voice
Coming from beyond
The disappearance of matter:

'We, Ion and Ioana,
By our own efforts,
Have founded this sacred
Child
For the eternal remembrance
Of this sun,
Of this earth.'

DEVELOPING

Today I photographed only trees
Ten, a hundred, a thousand,
I'll develop them at night
When the soul is a dark room.
Then I'll sort them
According to leaves, according to circles,
According to their shadows.
Oh, how easily
Trees merge one into another!
Look, there's only one left.
That one I'll photograph again
And then observe with terror
It resembles me.
Yesterday I photographed only stones
And the last stone
Resembled me.
The day before yesterday – chairs –
And the one that was left
Resembled me.

Everything is so much
Like me . . .

I'm afraid.

FEAR

Wherever I go
I take my body with me,
Because I've nowhere to leave it.
The earth, the sky,
And the water steal it.

In happiness, in love,
In sadness, and in agony,
I must feel my hands and forehead close to me,
I must feel my heart beating
Otherwise I worry.

We tremble, the way we tremble,
For the earth of our body,
Not yet too evolved,
From which after every shower
Worms still appear.

VISION

They no longer exist – new children,
The same parents from the beginning of the world
Continually give birth to the same children,
Who would realize the deception
If given more time.

But they're already born with moustaches
And have only the last
Seven days to live,
In which they stay rigid
In flesh and bone
As in the suits
Of astronauts.

And people really believe
That their sons will go
On an extraordinary journey
And they bring them flowers,
Which they neither see nor smell,
Because, look, they only have one day left
Out of seven.

The moment of launching approaches,
Children, be old,
Be rigid in your flesh and bone,
We'll launch you into the earth
With such great ceremony.

Even if we never receive
A single telegram from you,
At night we'll hear in sleep
The hurtling of your bodies,
Passing through each stratum,
Until when, on the other side of the planet,
Tired and blinded by darkness
You rise
In the womb of another woman.

A woman like any other woman,
Who believes that she loves,
That the child she suckles is hers,
And who, in her turn, has buried with flowers
Many children
For birth on the other hemisphere.

PRAYER

Saints,
Let me join your ranks
At least as an extra.

You're getting old,
Perhaps you feel the pain of age
Painted on your bodies
In so many stages.

Let me carry out
The humblest jobs
In nooks and crannies.

I could for instance,
Eat the light
At the Last Supper,
And blow out your haloes
When the service is over.

And, from time to time,
At half a wall's distance,
Cup my hands to my mouth
And holler, once for the believers
And once for the unbelievers:
Hallelujah! Hallelujah!

THE ROBOTS

Rust was going from house to house
Looking for people of iron.
In the morning
They had to extricate each other
With a hook
From under the wreckage of the rust.

That's why people don't want
To be made of iron any more.

And I have seen whole groups
Of mechanical ones
Who, sick of every type of car,
Are turning back to the age-old flesh
On foot.

LOOK . . .

Look . . . objects
Are cut in two,
On one side – the objects,
On the other – their names.

There is a vast space between them,
Space for running,
For life.

Look, you are cut in two.
On one side there's you,
On the other your name.

Don't you sometimes feel, maybe in dream,
Maybe near to dream,
That over your forehead
Other thoughts superimpose,
Over your hands
Other hands?

Someone understood you for a moment
Making your name
Pass through your body,
Painful and sonorous,
Like a bronze tongue
Through the emptiness of a bell.

ATAVISM

Looking out of the window has become a nervous tic,
Everyone's looking out of the window.
They read, they wash, they love, die,
And from time to time they rush
To look out of the window.

What do you want to see?
Who are you staring at?
Stop thinking about it, who's coming's come,
Who had to go's gone,
What was to pass by, has passed by,
Leave the curtains,
Pull the blinds
And take your blood pressure yet again.

Having seen everything, – rain, wars,
Sun, moles, events,
Always repeated exactly the same,
I can't believe mankind seriously wants
To see anything else.
However there it is stuck to the window
With hollow eyes.

THE MOUNTAIN

I'm standing in for a paving stone,
I got here
By a regrettable misunderstanding,
Over me have passed
Small cars,
Lorries,
Tanks
And many kinds of feet.

Up to its axle I have felt the sun's light,
And the moon
At about midnight.

Clouds oppress me with their shadow,
And from heavy
And important events –
I've got blisters.

And although with great stoicism
I put up with
My granite fate,
I sometimes find myself screaming out:

Drive only on the roadway
Of my soul,
Barbarians!

THE MOUTH OF THE CRAB

When mankind emerged from the water
Covered in silt, algae and salt,
On the other shore there rose,
Climbing, one on the back of the other
And slithering into the sea,
Only to rise again with the next wave
Onto grass – the crabs.

Hideous, the crabs, ulcerous,
Legs like warts,
Green with scum and red,
Raging red on the belly.

The people began to leave
Attempting to adapt to the drying
Light of the sun,
So different from the water's light.
The crabs began scuttling
In the opposite direction,
Stilts beating time on the globe
As on the chest of a down-trodden man.

Then one day they met,
The first people with
The first crabs,
Each one face to face,
They'd been lifted by the armpits
And pulled into the stagnant water of the sea,
Back over the places they'd been before
(Their eyes remembered them well
By tears shaped like burial mounds.)
But for the crabs they were really
New places,
And they thought themselves right
In carrying them forwards.

Only in the water did the people regain their senses,
And struggled there before every creature
And those who got away
From the rusty iron pincers
Emerged exhausted onto the shore
Covered in silt, algae and salt.

Taking a deep breath, tired, they set off ahead,
Yet look, on the opposite shore,
Crawling from under the shadow of the planet's silt,
Terrifyingly the crabs appear,
Setting off in the opposite direction.

A WINDOW FACES US

A window faces us,
Which, using both hands, we're forever
Wiping of rain.
Only we wipe it from the inside,
While the rain beats against it
From the other side,
And it's always misted, our window,
By an unknown tongue.

After a while we change the place.
Thinking our location's not so good,
We begin to wipe the window from further away.
Daily, the same movement
As servants
In a house of enigmas.

With eyes on the window, glued to the window,
We lift a thought like a pensive finger to the forehead.
And outside it's raining with a steady drumming,
And it's misty . . .

DANTE

The Divine Comedy, wandering pyramid,
Slightly inclined towards eternity,
I hear it at night when there's a moon
Gliding gently on the sand,
A millimetre a year this way and that
Without any hurry.

And inside,
Tightly sealed as if in himself
Is the Pharoah.

On his own he embalmed all those he knew,
From close acquaintance and from heresay,
Plunging his hand
Further than the white stones of antiquity.
How terrible to have a mortal world about you!
And he embalmed them
So as not to be alone in eternity too.
Everything that took place on earth
He crammed into his ark.

Nine heavens of sins, nine of waiting,
Nine of illusion,
All full to the brim.
And in their midst sits
Dante.

He observes hell, purgatory and heaven,
And when he gets bored, switches the signs,
The one in hell for heaven
And vice versa.
And he goes on doing it time after time,
So that all poor mortals
Haven't a clue where they stand.

But Dante keeps quiet till his veins swell
Pushing that pyramid from within,
Which advances slowly on the sand
A millimetre a year this way or that
Without any hurry.

THE RECKONING

There comes a time
When we have to draw a line under us
A black line
To do the summing up.

The few moments when you were about to be happy,
The few moments when we were nearly beautiful,
The few moments when we were almost a genius,
Occasionally we've met
Mountains, trees, water
(Whatever happened to them? Do they still exist?)
Each adds up to a brilliant future —
Which we've lived.

A woman we've loved,
Plus the same woman who didn't love us
Equals zero.

A quarter of a year of studies
Makes several million fodder words
Whose wisdom we've gradually eliminated.
And finally, a fate
Plus another fate (Now where does that come from?)
Equals two (Write one, carry one,
Perhaps, who knows, there is a life hereafter).

SIMPLE MECHANICS

He made up his mind
To move the universe
From one side to the other –
To earn his living.

Nothing more simple,
Around his temple –
A crown of imaginary lines,
Magnetic lines.
If you once chew through chaos
Goats hooves stick to them,
Birds catch them with beaks,
And seas wrap round
The hull of the tide.

You could see him passing through things,
Weighing his world,
Hung with bats' claws
On his imaginary lines.

However, after a star,
He started shedding leaves and plants,
Though he never took a wrong step,
Going the same way as the world's beginning,
Except that his halo didn't help him anymore,
The muscles of the magnet had a temperature.

In the meantime the universe had reached its position,
It's old position,
And he had to move it somewhere else
To earn his living.

And everything starts again from the beginning
And everthing's in motion.

THE MENU

In the morning, a thin slice of living
With butter.
We also have water which rises continuously
(Last night it took up three quarters
Of the surface of the globe)
And we quickly boil off all its microbes.

At lunch, we eat heartily and substantially –
Three sorts of earth:
Clay, sand and peat.

In the evening we don't often cook anything to eat.

We have a bite
Of perhaps a star plus a little honey,
Or something else which hasn't run out,
Happiness (Which in fact we're keeping for Sunday)
And anything else that might come about.

SKITTLES

Without doubt, the earth
Is a great
Bowling alley.

Because there aren't enough
Trees,
People stand
As well.

Someone throws the ball
From far away
And marks with chalk
Those who fall.

It's a society game
Of course,
Just as fine
As duelling.

It's all worked out in advance
With very great precision,
Only we, who are naive,
Keep going to the surgery.

Listen to the stars clattering
Back on the conveyor belt,
Tonight they'll be up on the horizon again.

SOLEMNLY

All my papers
I've carried in my arms
To a large field,
I've sown them solemnly
And ploughed them in
Deeply.

To see what will come
From these thoughts,
From joy, from sadness, happiness,
Winter, Spring, Summer and Autumn.

Now I'm walking
On the bare field
Hands behind my back,
More worried every day . . .

And yet it just can't be.
At least one word should have been good!

I'm positive that one day
This field will fill with flames
And I shall pass through them, solemnly
Crowned like Nero.

THE GIFT

– I'll prove to you that all these paintings are fakes,
Said the specialist, taking out the magnifying glass
He had just received as a gift
From the planet Mars.

The idea amused him, so the collector smiled,
By his canvases one could
Identify masterpieces anywhere in the world.
He'd spent the fortunes of a few generations on them,
Past and future.

– Let's begin from right to left,
Now look at this Titian!
Indeed through the lens the clumsiness of execution could
be seen,
The picture had been painted by an untalented pupil
During a lesson in drawing.

– Well, deep down I had my doubts about it.
The collector whispered, palely,
But the Raphael you're examining now,
If that's a copy
It was made by God's own hand. Ha, ha, ha!

– Look, said the inspector, who didn't feel like joking,
Showing him the registered serial number
In the Madonna's eyes.

By the time he reached the centre of the room,
he'd hardly turned
The lens towards them
When the paintings started falling of their own accord.

Before the last painting, Rembrandt the millionaire! –
the collector
Put his hand to his heart and falling
Bats flew from his mouth.

The specialist then passed through many galleries
On which he poured scorn.

Not even the frames were authentic,
The unyielding glass brought to light
Some appalling work.

All the great masters had been murdered
From their first strokes of the brush
And the killers stole their names,
Continuing to paint with their oils,
Which, together with the real blood,
Had died.

And so the galleries emptied,
Ignorant purchasers were placed in prison.
Behind the man with the magnifying glass a deadly waste was
                                                        stretching
And he grew increasingly sad.

Then it occurred to him,
To turn the lens to the street where he walked,
And he noticed with amazement that it too was a fake.
The real street was much further away.
He looked at the town – a fake, the trees, fakes,
And he began to cry.

Sobbing and shaking all over,
Except for the hand holding the fearful instrument,
Now very old, he set off ahead,
Continuing to demolish the world.

TOYS

The likes of us, so very grown up
Who haven't fallen on ice
Since between the wars,
Or if in error, we toppled over,
Fractured a year as well.
One of those important years, rigid
With plaster . . .
Oh, though very grown up, there's still
That feeling
Of missing our toys.

We have all we need,
But we miss the toys.
We long for the optimism
Of cotton-hearted dolls
And for the clipper
With its three tiered sails,
Which goes as well on water
As it does on land.

We'd love to ride a rocking horse
And with all its wood, just once hear it neigh,
And then we'd say, "Take us someplace,
No matter where,
Because everywhere in life
We're determined to achieve
Some extraordinary deeds."

Oh, sometimes, how we miss the toys!
Yet can't be miserable
Because of it,
Can't sob from the bottom of our hearts
Holding with our hands the leg of the table,
Because we're such grown up people
And there's no one left that's older
To soothe away our fears.

WHO

We must check well
Who is hiding within us,
Let's be very careful
Who we're calling
Me . . .

Because we can no longer
Trust anyone
Blindly,
Let's be careful, especially
Who we're calling
Me.

Having crammed with a knee
Under such conventional masks,
Laughter, crying, love –
We strive clumsily
To be familiar with ourselves.

We might even succeed
Sometimes,
Yet we get so frightened
When we hear our own voice.

A STRAW

A straw spent all its youth
In a mattress
And thought the world
To have only one dimension:
Weight.

Daily it pressed
With a force equal to desperation.
How do you know how it feels
You, who haven't spent all your youth
In a mattress?!

Now it goes quite mad,
The nights are as light
As the days,
Not even the dust settles on it
To rest for two hours after dinner.

It's as if it wasn't a straw anymore,
But a feather from an angel's wing –
A former neighbour from the mattress –
That's how light it feels.

Yet sometimes intuition tells him
That, after all, the sky's also a mattress,
A bluer one,
On which the master snores.

EVERYONE

The old ones and the dead
Are like a tonic,
It's comforting to watch them.
It's they who are old not us,
They fulfill the act of death
Not us.

Most children
Are started
After some sudden death,
After, who knows who's funeral
Lovers feel a mad urge
To be alive.

And when no one
Departs this earth,
People watch the sky, worried.
If a star should fall
It means they can make their bed
In peace.

Everyone should ask himself,
I wonder who died
When I was born?

SYMMETRY

I was walking
When suddenly two roads opened
In front of me;
One to the right,
And one to the left,
Conforming to all the rules of symmetry.

I stopped,
Screwed up my eyes,
Pursed my lips,
Coughed,
And set off on the one to the right
(Just the one I shouldn't have taken
As was proved later.)

I went on as best I could,
No need to give details.
And then in front of me opened two
Precipices:
One to the right,
One to the left.
I threw myself into the left one,
Without even blinking, or jumping,
Just like a big heap into the one on the left,
Which, unfortunately, wasn't lined with feathers!
Crawling, I set off again.
I crawled for some time,
And suddenly in front of me
Two wide roads opened.
"I'll show you!" – I told myself,
And with grim determination,
I set off again on the one to the left.
Wrong, very wrong, the one on my right
Was the proper one, the real road, the great road.
And at the first crossroads
I gave myself totally
To the one on the right. Then the same again,
The other should have been the one, the other . . .

Now the food's almost gone,
My walking stick's aged,
Its buds no longer appear
So I can rest in their shade
When I become desperate.
Stones wear out my bones,
They creak and grumble at me
For one mistake after another . . .

And look, in front of me, opening again
Two skies:
One to the right,
One to the left.

THE CAMEL

How many times was it just about
To pass through
The eye of the needle!
How many times was it just about
To be sucked into the eye of the needle,
Dangerously deep.

Now it goes over whole fields of needles,
It steps calmly on spines, and spikes, new needles, needles,
The camel moves on,
Minding its own road, its own thirst,
Wise camel
Who carries us on his back
Us, the ones with the desert.

THE RUNNER

A deserted field,
Trodden down like a road,
And here and there
A book.

At great distances,
A basic book.
Firm as a rock.

Someone is coming, panting with muscles,
Healthy as a new god,
And spits on it,
On each one in a row,
Steps on them heavenly.

He tires, he's had enough,
The field stretches ahead, deserted,
Trodden down like a road,
The runner collapses, dies,
Becomes a basic book, the last word,
A sign over which one cannot pass anymore.

Panting is heard,
From beyond a figure appears,
A runner stops, spits on the sign
And disappears over the horizon.

FRIENDS

Let's commit suicide, I said to my friends,
Today we've really understood each other,
We've been very depressed,
Never again will we reach
Such a peak of perfection
And it's a pity to waste the opportunity.

I think the bathroom's the most tragic place,
Let's do it like the enlightened Romans
Who opened their veins
While discussing the essence of love,
Look, I've warmed the water,
Let's make a start, dear friends, I'll count to three.

In hell I was somewhat surprised to find myself alone.
Perhaps some people don't die quite so easily
I told myself, or have ties,
I couldn't have made a mistake: making a pact must mean
                                        something.
But time went on . . .

I can assure you, it was quite hard for me in hell,
Especially at the start, as I was on my own,
There was no one there I could talk to,
But gradually I was accepted, made friends.

A very tightly knit group,
We discussed all sorts of theoretical questions,
We felt great,
We even got around to suicide.

And again I found myself alone, in purgatory
Looking for a few kindred spirits,
Although the purgatorians were quite suspicious –
With their uncertain situation
Between two worlds –
A girl loves me, she's very beautiful.
We share moments of great ecstasy – unbelievable, fantastic!

45

And I almost feel like saying to her . . .
But having seen it all before, I let her do it first,
I wait and commit suicide afterwards,
Yet the girl somehow manages to come back to life –
And then I'm on my own in heaven –
No one's ever reached that far before,
I'm the first, the world exists only as a project,
Something very, very vague
In God's head,
I'm getting very friendly with him lately.

There's sadness at all levels,
Even God's desperate,
I look into his empty eyes and lose myself there.
He slips roaring down the precipice of my deaths,
We understand each other perfectly,
God, I think we've reached perfection,
You first,
How about leaving it all in the dark?

* * *

I'm sorry for the butterflies
When I switch the light off,
And for the bats
When I switch it on . . .
Can't I move an inch
Without offending anyone?

So many strange things happen,
That I could always stay
Head in hands,
But an anchor thrown from heaven
Pulls them down . . .

The time isn't yet ripe
To rip the canvases,
Leave it.

THE ACTORS

How easy going – the actors!
With their sleeves rolled up
How cleverly they're able to be us!

I've never seen a more perfect kiss
Than by actors in the third act,
When emotions are beginning
To clear.

Stained with oil
In authentic caps,
Carrying out all kinds of jobs,
They enter and exit on lines
Which roll from their feet like rugs.

So natural is their death on stage
That, compared to this perfection,
The ones in the graveyards
Seem to move,
Those who wear forever the make-up of tragedy,
The real dead!

We're stiff and awkward in just one life!
We don't know how to live it properly anyway.
We talk a load of nonsense or keep silent years on end,
And embarrassed and unattractive
We don't know what the hell to do with our hands.

CARBON PAPER

At night someone puts on my door
A huge carbon paper,
And all my thoughts appear, instantaneously
On the outside of the door.

The curious ones from all over the world
Rush towards my house,
I hear them going up the stairs,
Taking the steps on their soles
And replacing them
As they leave.

They are birds of every species,
Guard dogs of the moon,
Passageways
And old acacias
Suffering from insomnia.

They put on their glasses
And read me with emotion
Or threaten with their fists,
Because about everything I have formed
A clear idea.

Only about my soul
Nothing's known,
My soul which always escapes me
Through the days,
Like a piece of soap
In the bath.

ALCHEMY

Ninety nine elements,
Gather, fuse together, separate,
Give me happiness.

Ninety nine elements,
I give you half my brow,
Arrange youselves now,
So much iron, so much gold, so much mercury –
And give me happiness.

Ninety nine elements,
Your calculations make no sense,
They've left only wisdom,
Give me happiness.

Ninety nine elements,
What shall I do with such disillusion
In the shape of a star, youth, a woman,
And other ideals –
Give me happiness.

Ninety nine elements,
Shown on the chart of my existence,
Look I fling beneath your cauldron a day,
Another year,
Another age . . .

OUT OF REACH

This woman
Has someone in the bathroom.

She talks to me,
She loves me sincerely,
But in her soul, someone always fidgets
Just out of reach.
I read in her eyes,
Her hair,
In the life of her palm,
That this house has only one entrance,
And that she's hiding someone from me, in the bathroom.

Or, in the house next door,
Or a different house,
Somewhere in the street,
Another town, a forest,
Or even on the bottom of the sea.

Someone stays hidden there,
Preying upon my thoughts,
Listening to my eternal feelings
With one eye on the clock.

DON JUAN

When he'd finished eating tons of lipstick,
The women,
Robbed of their most holy expectations,
Discovered a way to revenge themselves
On this Don Juan.

Each morning,
Before the mirror,
When they've pencilled in their eyebrows,
They draw on lips
With pesticide,
Spray pesticide on hair,
On white shoulders, in eyes, on thoughts,
On tits,
And wait.

They appear, white on balconies,
Look for him in parks,
But Don Juan, as if forewarned,
Has become the book worm of the library.

He caresses only rare editions,
Or perhaps paperbacks,
But never a volume bound in skin.
The dust on the classics
Now seems more refined to him
Than the perfume of the bedroom.

And they await him.
Poisoned in all five senses – they wait,
And if Don Juan would raise his eyes
From his new passion,
He would see through the window of the library,
How a loving husband is buried daily,
Killed in action,
While in error
Kissing his wife.

THE CLOUDS

I'm looking up,
At the clouds which rush backwards to me,
Always backwards.

First
The trees in them collapse towards me,
Towns crumble towards me,
Rivers flow cascading over me,
And from above the harvest falls,
Beating rhythmically on the drum of my belly.

I'm looking up,
Straight up,
As if from the bottom of a precipice
At the white clouds,
Through which stars like blobs of fat
Float as in soup.

The world flows above me;
Looking up like this
I've covered the best part
Of it.

THE LESSON

Every time I'm called to the front
I answer every question
In a muddle.

– How are you getting on with History?
My teacher asks.
– Badly, very badly,
I've just made a lasting peace
With the Turks.

– What is the law of gravity?
– Wherever we find ourselves,
On water or on land,
On the ground or in the air,
Everything's bound to fall
Upon our heads.

– What stage of civilization
Have we reached?
– The era of rough stones,
Because the only polished one
Ever found,
The heart,
Has been lost.

– Can you draw the map of our highest hopes?
– Yes, with coloured balloons.
With each stronger gust
Another balloon flies.

From all this it's clear
I'll have to stay down a year,
And rightly so.

LEVERS

So heavy is my soul
It's as if God's hanging there to pull
Down like a boulder on the balance of a well's lever.
I am his darkness from which miracles emerge
And I am the world's precursor.

A star sets out further,
Keep away from it, don't move nearer,
Look it's creaking on my breath,
Should anything stop its path
For me it could mean death.

Out of my soul rise mountains with horizons that fall,
Like stoics on nails of the fir tree,
Sometimes a cloud will gush
From a pore that dilates too much,
But more often it's a sea of salt.

I transmit myself forever in the distance
In that thousandth appearance.
Like a long-armed lever
Life from death I can sever.

Everywhere in the world I'm spread,
Thinking it over and thinking it out,
But like a well, by the universe I'm drained
At the week's end.

THIEVES

I had a poem which wouldn't let me sleep
And I sent it into the country
To a grandfather.

Eventually I wrote another
And sent it to my mother
To store in the loft.

After these I wrote some more
And, with a heavy heart entrusted them to relatives,
Who promised to look after them.

And the same for each new poem,
A good soul was found to receive it.
Because each friend of mine
Has in turn a friend,
So true he can entrust him with the secret.

So that even I no longer know
The resting place of a particular verse
And should thieves break in,
No matter how much they torture me,
I couldn't tell them more, than
That they're in a safe place,
Somewhere in this country.

THE MAXIMUM DURATION

Surrendered to the world
We live hands up,
That's why we can't do anything.
Our hands are caught by fear, surrendering.

Wasted to the world –
Death – a possibility to close up
One's self,
To empty space to make room for yet another.
Huddled, crouched, a hedgehog,
The mind changes is mind, the possibility.

In a way only death
Makes a man of you, rids you of others,
You live in the world, but you die
Within yourself.
It's an immense triumph: this conquering
Of self, and as in any victory, destroying
What you've conquered.

THE TWO THIEVES

The two thieves are important
As well.
One stole a candle stick,
The other beat up an animal.
Yet they too are important.
What a great thief
Is the one in the middle,
He's stolen all our glory!
If he'd not had so much publicity,
Perhaps there'd have been some left for us,
Us crucified more awry.

IF IT'S NOT ASKING TOO MUCH

– What would you take with you,
If the question ever arose
That you should commute daily between Heaven and Hell,
To give some lectures?

– A book, a bottle of wine and a woman, God,
If it's not asking too much.

– You do ask too much, we'll cut out the woman,
She'd keep you talking,
She'd cloud your mind with nonsense
And you'd never be able to prepare your lectures.

– I implore you to cut out the book,
I'll write one, God, as long as I've got near me
A bottle of wine and a woman.
That's what I'd like, if it's not asking too much.

– You are asking too much.
What would you like to take with you,
If the question ever arose
That you should commute daily between Heaven and Hell
To give some lectures?

– A bottle of wine and a woman,
If it's not asking too much.
– You've already asked that, why are you so stubborn?
It's too much. I tell you, we'll cut out the woman.

– What have you got against her, why the persecution?
Better to cut out the wine,
It makes me sleepy and I wouldn't be able to prepare my lectures,
With inspiration gained from the eyes of my love.

Silence, long minutes,
Maybe even eternities,
Allowing me time to forget.

– What would you like to take with you,
If the question ever arose
That you should commute daily between Heaven and Hell
To give some lectures?

– A woman, God, if it's not asking too much.
– It is asking too much, we're cutting out the woman.
– Better to cut out the lectures,
Cut out the Hell and the Heaven,
It's either all or nothing.
I'd be commuting between Heaven and Hell in vain.
How else can I frighten and terrify sinners in Hell,
If I haven't got a woman, visual aid, to show them?
How can I raise the righteous to Heaven
If I haven't got the book to enlighten them?
And how can I put up with the journey and the differences
In temperature, luminosity and pressure
Between Heaven and Hell.
If I haven't got the wine to give me courage?

PERPETUUM MOBILE

However, Prometheus was left the right to reply.
But while transfixed upon the rock,
Motionless, torn only from within,
The only line he said was this:
– Why the liver?

Of course in appearance the simplest
And most banal of lines
– Why the liver?
He had in his head a whole speech
About the value of fire
And the extraordinary dignity of this gesture of Titanical revolt.

A very well-knit speech which would have held artistically too,
And which he wanted to scream out defiantly at Zeus,
But found himself uttering only this:
– Why the liver?

On his left, hungry, the vulture's very fierce,
He's good at his job, he's openly a henchman,
Has a beak like an excavator,
Which piercing makes the mountains rumble
With these almost onomatopoeic words
– That's why!'

This is and is not an answer
To the question devouring the hero,
Who, forgotten by the world in the rocky wilderness of the
Caucasus,
Still makes the horizons hoarse
Using his sacred right of reply.
– Why the liv-er-er-er?

REMEDY

When the remedy for an illness is found
All those who died of that illness
Should come alive again
And continue to live
The rest of their days
Until taken ill by another illness
For which there is yet no cure.

ULYSSES

And when I think of what's waiting for me at home,
Those pigs of suitors
Blind drunk, filthy armour on the hall stand,
Playing backgammon all day long,
Until muscle and dice flag all in a heap.
They're certainly no good for marriage
Not even to an old crone,
Let alone Penelope
(Could she really have aged that fast as well?)
And on the other hand that woman who whines,
And can't stop weaving due to nerves,
Who, because she's a witch, is surely the one to muddle up the
                                        world's strings!
I can see her now pouncing from the gate:
– Where have you been all this time?
– Don't be a shrew – I fought the Trojan war . . .
– All right, all right, but that Agamemnon of Clytemnestra
How did he manage to get away earlier, so that by now he's
                                        actually rotted,
Didn't you all fight the same war?
– For ten years I've been wandering at sea, because Neptune . . .
– Leave Neptune out of it, and tell me straight, who were
                                        you with?
And all this time!
And all this time!
And what sort of sea was it anyway?

Oh, if only I could build myself a little house
Here on the waves,
Raise a tent in this little corner
So isolated
Between Scylla and Charybdis.

ERRATUM TO HEAVEN

Instead of Adam and Eve please read so and so.
In the end we'll have to give another erratum to the erratum:
So and so isn't so and so.
The main thing is that I know
And you know,
Nothing else matters.
I know you love me,
You know I love you.
The rest is silence. Shh!
– That's what you think, you and Hamlet!
Everything's known,
Everyone's talking about it.
So what?

Italian light music
Is the only stuff worth listening to,
Yet even for that I haven't developed a taste,
Our life's not long enough
To live everything to the full.
Sometimes you feel the same way too,
I accept that,
Yet at other times even this life seems too long.

We dilate the moment
And enter there
As into the frame of an old family photograph.
The man and the woman of uncerain age,
However still young,
He catches her hand,
And can sense something fluttering there,
At the level of the hand a flutter of an eyelid.
How true when you said
You could see me with your palms,
When you let them caress my trail
In the air which for a time you dispelled
So that I suffocated with your presence
(It was me who said that).
And the lady looks at the camera,

64

But the moment already has an old frame,
Carved in wood, with little flowers,
And both the man and the woman,
Dressed in their best, but not traditional dress from Paradise,
– Do you remember 'Adam and Eve' by Cranach? –
With a tie and a collar with frills.
And on each side of them the moment,
As I was saying.

You can't place beauty behind bars,
For it can open anything,
Anyone could let it out.
What's that got to do with clothes?
Anyway I love your velvet dress,
So does my palm, the bridge of my palm
Which charms it with love
As a bridge does over a fine path,
Even my palm seems made from velvet
Velvet upon velvet, we yearn for it!
As a present for today I'm giving you
These words,
Instead of a bunch of carnations,
With three sprigs of fern.

DEEPLY CEREBRAL

Deeply cerebral is the fog
From the brain, at seven in the morning,
(Well, half past seven) after that it humanizes a little,
Clears a bit,
A haze of chaos in which new forms are shaping
On a melody which flows . . .Now which one is it? 'God knows!'

As we got dressed in this state of fusion,
This downpour of angels,
Spindles of smoke dripping in stanzas,
The soul in holes – hexagons, hexagons,
A honeycomb for smoke.
The smoke's our honey.
The honeycomb presumes a melody the soul touches
Perfecting, making it geometrical.
'Nose to the gems, it passes' . . .
'Just observe such abstract prowess.'

I missed you like a trajectory in a void, in longing,
Dressed in decoration, in any way,
I simply missed you, the way you are, *tale quale*.
I got used to passing there
On that trajectory
And with you the void seemed heavy
With astral beauty.

Doesn't anyone understand that only when scraped of
rose- coloured lights
Can the poetry of love return to its origins
And start again with renewed energy from the beginning . . . ?
'Are you telling me?' 'You, – anyone,'
But no one listens, you see!

THE TRAY OF EMBERS

Imagine that we lived
Three thousands years ago, so today
Everything is part of the past.
I'd be part of the past.
You'd be part of the past
And yet they wouldn't even learn about us in History
Because they don't teach you about love.
One passes over great love affairs.
No one dog-ears the pages. Or makes a mark –
So it's better anonymous and in bed
Than anonymous and long since dead!
Oh, does it rhyme? Only a little bit, for you
I'm making concessions to fixed forms,
To your fixed form.
You must inspire me to write rhymes,
Sonnets, rhythms and rondels –
Don't keep coming to me with a tray of inspiration
All spilt.
You can rest it on your breast, because there it stays,
It still stays,
That, in fact, is the tray of embers,
For the winged horse with one wing
Burnt (It's been a time of burning
But it's healed now.)
Lips, the roof of the mouth, wings, fingers –
Everything's passed through the fire.
You know, this red
Makes you look quite in tune with the times.
And one can see you're dark under the auburn.
Why do you like to be layered like that?
Instead of answering, you take my palm.
"Oh! You're going to have a long life. You'll bury all of us!
And the luck line's parallel with the life line."
"So I'll be unlucky in the hereafter then?"
You have a hand like a linnet's
Whose nest is there as well.
All your luck lines are made of feathers

And your life line is like a straw.
But long, so long you can even play it.
Straw pipes. Pipes of straw (to be prosaic)
On which my spirit ruminates.
Your life line has echoes in other lives.

SYMPHONY

Your body has incredible fingering,
Like an undiscovered cave in me it's always resounding.
Blocked at its mouth by a rock where Prometheus
Lies transfixed (yes, it has to be Prometheus).
Because I feel the warmth, the punished shouting 'Fire! Fire!'
And I hear the engine 'Where's the fire? Where's the fire?'
But it goes away, because they're not designed to put out livers.

And inside, behind the curtain of pain
Am I, a projection of the one on the outside . . .
I hope that's not too hard for you . . . Do you realize that the
                                              crucified,
Enchained one is also me . . . that your indifference has
                                              detached me,
Breaking me into two equal parts.
And my double's in the cave . . . a man of snows,
Tightly enclosed, yet even that far
The keyboard of your body still resounds,
Because that's where I began . . .
So bang your head against the walls,
Put your ear to icicles, stalactites
(It's always me who does it),
Trying to hear all that divine music, there in the darkness,
What you say, what you think, how you walk,
Trying in vain to turn the music louder on your network.
Silence. Inside I eat ice,
Outside I burn consumed by flames
Then suddenly, you, with your heavenly keyboard.
Piano for ribs, violin under your arm, silver bells
And a percussion instrument . . .

But this can change absolutely nothing,
Neither in the cave, nor on the rock which bars the entrance
Where my thirst for you burns up . . .
I tell you all this.
To translate for you in an articulate language, a number of
                                              age old feelings
You don't even know what intense feelings
And classical performances you give me . . .

THE SEASON AND THE DEAD

It's an autumn which wakes the dead
At the crack of dawn,
At the crack of doom.
Well, it will wake them, if you want it to,
And turn them over
Together with this year's leaves.

FASTING

Friday's here again, I can't eat meat again.
Perhaps sturgeon? Sturgeon's awful.
A campari?
I've also got a nervous fluttering in my stomach.
There's nothing wrong with you, a slight bout of hypocondria,
In the stomach? In the head, but it reaches the stomach
When I think the weather's changing.

I'm very sensitive to the day's metamorphosis,
Each hour moves me in a certain way,
Gets in touch with one certain nerve.
And I'm also sensitive about
What's written in the paper, or on the window, or on the pavement
with chalk.

We fuss over each other.
Do you want a yoghurt? Have a yoghurt,
So that we can live our ripe old age now, in intervals,
Like they serve yoghurts at boxing matches,
Between the rounds.
They don't serve yoghurt there.
Well anyway, something healthy, non-alcoholic,
So you only get punched in an optimal state,
Isn't colitis in the oesophagus? In the ears.
Then I need – something to soothe my hearing,
Say a magic word to me.

SUNSET Opus No 15

How weary is my ear
When it no longer hears you.
Music is noise without you
(A sonnet verse, put it on one side,
What do you expect, I can't break with tradition,
Just like that, at the drop of a hat.
The classic in me constantly echoes,)
And everything's a whistled prayer one can dance to.

We are the eighth day unfaithful ones.
("Monday?") No, we invent a day,
Pull the week by its ends to squeeze out one more day.
Love dilates, didn't you know?
Time, space, everything.
The earth swells with love, while we love, the others
The nameless ones, the multitude, amassed,
Bulging like a beautiful womb
And the solar system says (or another lunar or stellary system)
'Look, such a round shape is happiness in the universe.
It's fortunate orbits can be corrected this way,
Or terra firma might end up in hell in the sterility
Where everything floats.'
I heard this said word for word
While watching a sunset such as this.
The sun sets again descending under lightning conductors,
Squeezing down some house chimney –
Just the way you cling to me like cellotape,
Ah! those fertile embraces!
What an example we'd set in the ether.

We, the eighth day unfaithful ones,
Who alone stretch the blanket of time,
Inventing for themselves this day to end each week,
Creating it from cuttings of other days,
From Tuesday, a little bit of Wednesday, something from
                                        Thursday,
And let's steal a little bit of Friday as well,
And look there's another day.
A day on the side,
It exists, it exists, but only we know.

72

* * *

When I want to have a rest
I'm ill.
I take to my bed.
Imagine how ill
I'll be
Dead!

SYNCHRONIZATION

Everything about us is perfect
On this century's
Cinema screen:
Both in sound and image.

It's just that many times
With appearance on cue,
We start to act and talk sense –
But nothing's heard.
Your words on the screen run ahead
Or get stopped at customs.
At other times you find yourself speaking
Someone else's lines,
Which don't fit your mouth,
You're too big or too small.

Then far worse
Is when your voice begins to be heard
After you've emerged
From the projector's beam
Of sun.

It doesn't matter.
There are a few small defects
Of synchronization.
Perhaps in time we'll be able
To say exactly what we think,
And to speak
Even in our lifetime.

SENTENCE

Each traveller in the tram
Looks identical to the one who sat there before him
On that very seat.

Either the speed's far too great,
Or the world's far too small.

Each has a threadbare neck caused
By the newspaper read behind him.
I'm aware of a newspaper in the neck
Turning and cutting my veins
With its edges.

COMPETITION

One, two, three . . .
The hibernation competition has begun.
Everyone lock yourselves in your lair
And let's see who can hibernate the longest.

You know the competition rules:
No moving,
No dreaming,
No thinking.
Anyone caught thinking
Is out of the game and no longer our concern.

Like a pipe, you can only use
Your paw for sucking
To stimulate you in the deep understanding
Of this event.

I'm lucky to find myself near a bear,
Because when I've had enough of my paw,
I'll give it to him,
And use his,
Which as it happens is within the accepted norm
Of paws.
And although the Pharoah Cheops
Has the advantage of a few milleniums,
I also hope to overtake him
By an outstanding sprint
Our famous sprint
In the field of hibernation.

THE TRAVELLER

The waters I've just come through
Have left a memory, a slight sheen under my skin,
I can't run nimbly with speed
Unless I have heels covered in blisters,
Unless they feel like a marsh,
Where you imperceptibly sink.

I can only fall asleep when I crouch
Somewhere on a suitcase near overcrowded
Train doors,
Woken from dozing everytime a passenger gets on
Or gets off.
In these breaks I dream the most beautiful dreams,
All, alas, interrupted abruptly.

Ah, sleep in an average, strange bed
In a third rate hotel!
One falls flat on the greasy divan, damp, slightly cock-eyed,
In the room there's a smell of prison,
The window's barred.
And it'd be stupid to open it because beggars can jump.

About midnight, pain wakes you,
It's in the ribs, made by the springs,
You feel your way and can't find the light.
Where are you? Which town is it?
You think you're still travelling and wait for the guard,
"What's the next station, please?"

Sometimes it's true, you're in the express!
In the sleeper. You decided to treat yourself.
At the window you recognise nothing,
The scenery may just as well
Be Italian, Swiss or even the moon.
Trees change from second to second.
Like guards of honour
At a hasty funeral,
Or like telegrams received in battle

Where the result's uncertain.
You're the commander, you received them, opened them,
The subalterns are watching your mouth waiting for orders,
But the telegrams are ciphered
And you've forgotten the cipher of the leaves.

I only feel well when
Half-asleep, uncomfortable,
Standing on one foot on a blister
Strap-hanging, hung on a window-sill,
On a servant's stair,
Having to rush urgently God knows where,
Carrying four big suitcases full of useless things,
Relinquishing, because of them, the only thing
Of any importance: the umbrella. (It always rains cats and dogs,
                                           when you're a traveller.)

I only feel well when unwell,
Limping,
Bags under the eyes,
Thrown in the street by my own anxiety . . .

Always pushed about on roads like a kick up the arse,
Eyes bulging, as if I'd seen a miracle.

THE INVISIBLE ONES

The royal throne is right there in my head,
Or to be more exact, it is my head,
It's all that's left
Of an area as vast as the eye can see.

And over it
How many invasions have spread,
How many trenches must I dig daily
To fill them all with sweat from my brow
– It's fresher, running, and much safer –
To raise turret walls round it.
And in the end defend it sword in hand.

Of course I fight the battle
With the barbarians.
As many as there are grains of sand,
Their numbers darken even the sun,
It's just that they can't be seen,
They're barbarians totally invisible,

That's why the battle's even more terrible
And even more a struggle for life and death,
It's just that I've no blood left to spill
Unless perhaps it's mine again
If I suddenly feel like suicide.

My one wish is that these efforts of mine
Be recorded in the struggle for independence,
And that important historical events
Be given their true significance.

* * *

Every year
Life salutes us
With 365 shots
Of sun.

It's a great event
Our arrival into
The inanimate world,
And matter
Gives us due
Honours.

The trees put on little flags
Of seasons,
In the air, oxygen bubbles rise
And coloured stars.

From the sea cheers are heard,
Waves carry banners.
Everything
Clamours to see us.
What more can I say?
It's a beautiful and unrivalled feast.

And we, moved,
For as long as the light lasts,
Stay standing
As for the national anthem.

WITH JUST ONE LIFE

Hold with both hands
The tray of each day
And pass in a line
In front of this counter.

There's enough sun
For everyone,
There's enough sky,
There's enough moon.

From the earth comes fragrance
Of luck, happiness, glory
Which tickles your nostrils
Temptingly.

So don't be miserly,
Live as your heart's stirred,
The prices are absurd.

For instance, with just one life
You can get
The most beautiful woman
And a wife. *

*Altered with permission of the author.

THE OLD ONES IN THE SHADE

You tire quickly, you forget easily,
You begin talking to yourself,
You move your lips . . .
In the mirror you catch yourself moving your lips.

I know roughly what it's going to be like when I'm old.
Every summer I experience one or two days a week
Of old age.
Wrinkled, dried out like a peach stone in the core
Of a juicy day.

A Ulysses with a mind like a sieve,
Forgetting where he was supposed to return,
Why he wanders on the sea
And whether it's before or after the Trojan wars.
A Ulysses with few chances of kissing the smoke
                                    leaving the chimneys
Of his homelands.

You hesitate whether to adjust your tie
Or strangle yourself with it.

40 degrees in the sun! I come into the house
And with a last mental effort remember
What I'm called.
The sultry heat resembles old age.
The same sensations.

The carpet slips from under your feet
You trip over your slippers –
A nail is turning purple.
You seem to have a wobbling tooth.

There's a feeling of unity in summer,
We're all older,
Even the foetus in the womb of the mother.

TRUTH COMES TO LIGHT

Truth comes to light
Extremely slowly.
Following the movement technique
Of decomposure and rotting
Oil rises to the surface,
But only after it's drowned.

LET'S TALK ABOUT THE WEATHER...

We've finished all topics of conversation,
Now let's talk about the weather.
Any one can say something
About weather.

I, to start talking,
Will be of the opinion it'll rain,
Because I dreamt of a big cloud
Circling round my brow
Which always rained on me,
Soaking thoughts to the skin.

Someone
To contradict me, insists upon good weather.
For in the following three centuries,
The sky will be so bright
That we'll all see each other
Without needing fireworks
To do so.

Someone talks to us about a dead leaf,
Which flies before the bare trees
And which none of us can keep —
Tomorrow it'll pass our street,
Let's go on the balcony
And watch it too.

And so we're able to hold a conversation,
We'll contradict each other and speak very loudly,
So that crickets inside us run away hurriedly.

The main thing is silence shouldn't come between us,
The main thing is to appear happy.